A PANGOLIN'S MANIFESTO

by RACHEL SHAW

It's not my fault

APOLLO
PUBLISHERS

To all those who want to roll into
a ball when life gets tough.

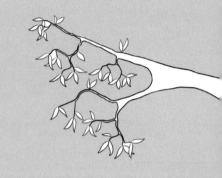

Have you ever gotten into trouble simply for hanging out with your friends?

No. Worse than that.

As bad as it gets.

The Savannah Post

Deadly virus may have jumped from bats to people via pangolins

DAILY LEAF

...angolins blamed

Forest Times

Pangolins linked to global pandemic

World goes into quarantine

When it feels like the whole world is against you, do you want to roll into a ball and hide?

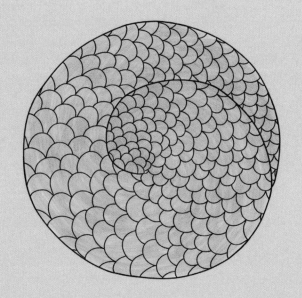

The world can be
a scary place.

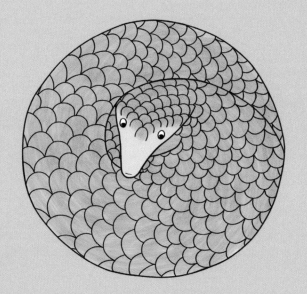

But the dangers you face
aren't always the same as
the things that you fear.

**Building your defenses
to the obvious threats
might make you vulnerable
to other threats . . .**

like being pango-napped . . .

It's estimated that a pangolin is snatched from the wild by human poachers every five minutes.

and shipped far away from home.

Pangolins are believed to be the world's most trafficked mammal, accounting for 20 percent of all illegal wildlife trade.

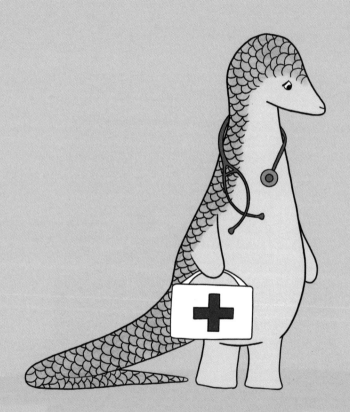

Despite the stories about pangolins spreading viruses to humans, there is a long-held belief that they can cure human ailments.

There is no evidence that pangolin scales have any medicinal value, yet they are used in traditional Chinese medicines.

Pangolin meat is an expensive delicacy that is sometimes served illegally by restaurants.

Pangolins are the only
mammals with scales.
Their scales are made
of keratin, like human
hair and fingernails.

The illegal wildlife trade threatens the survival of pangolins.

Bringing wild animals close to humans increases the risk of the transfer of viruses between species.

Life can be hard when
you're a pangolin.

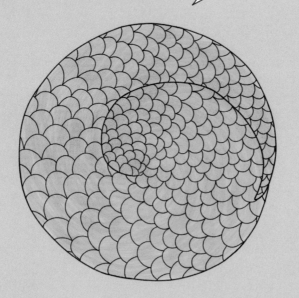

The safest thing to
do is stay home.

Make your home your favorite place to be. First, find a cozy spot in a hollow tree . . .

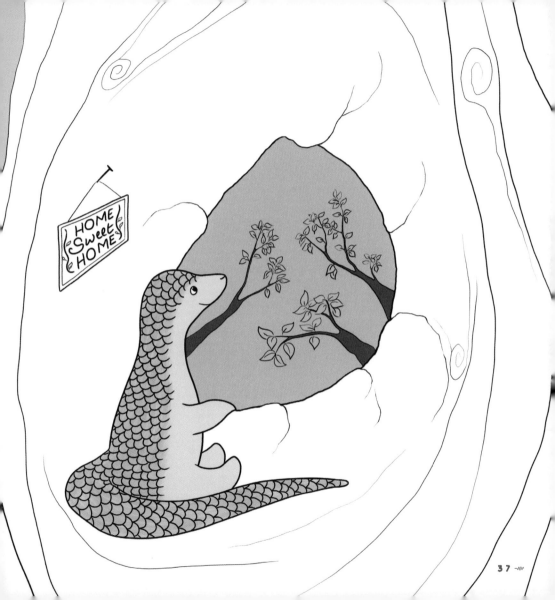

or even in
an aardvark's
burrow.

You never know who you might meet in an aardvark's burrow. Painted dogs, porcupines, warthogs, honey badgers, and pangolins all find shelter in them.

Snuggle in your own
sanctuary of solitude.

Sleeping well is vital if you're going to be
ready to greet the new day . . . or night,
if you're nocturnal like a pangolin.

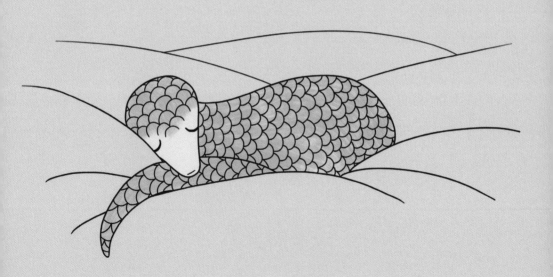

When you're home
alone, remember
you can sing . . .

there's no one
listening.

Pangolins are quiet animals with very few vocalizations. No one knows if they sing while they are alone.

Or dance . . .

there's no one's watching.

Make sure you've got plenty to read.

When you read, you can go on adventures without leaving home.

Pangolins have poor eyesight.
(And there's no evidence that
pangolins can read.)

Release your
inner creativity.

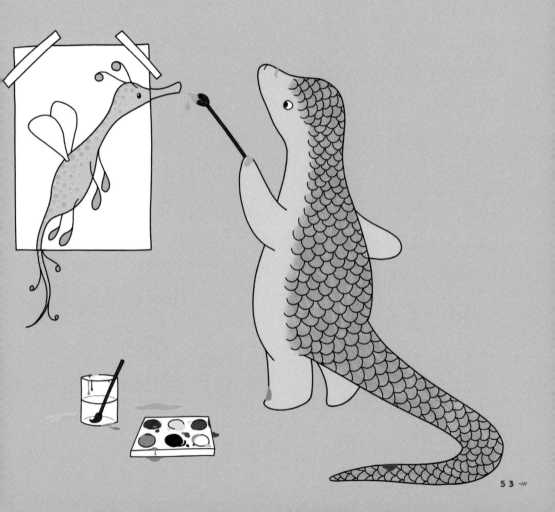

Wash away your worries
as you wash away the
dirt of the day.

If you don't have bubbles, try mud.

Pangolins don't need an expensive spa day—a roll in mud cools them down and helps remove parasites.

Beware the transfixing power of screens.

If you're a pangolin, you shouldn't know the word "television."

When you feel overwhelmed by choice, keep it simple . . .

enjoy a myrmecophagous diet.

Three hundred grams of ants a day is enough food for the average pangolin, but they must also swallow some stones to help break down the critters' exoskeletons once they reach the pangolin's stomach.

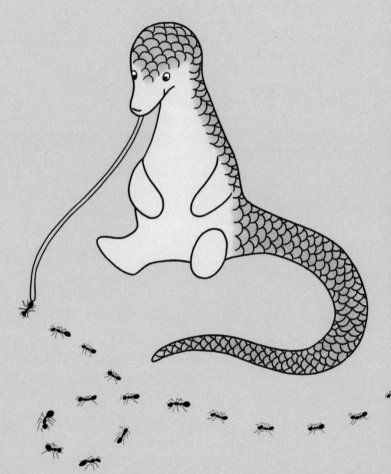

It will help you maintain a healthy weight.

A pangolin's scales make up 20 percent of its body weight.

Exercise daily.

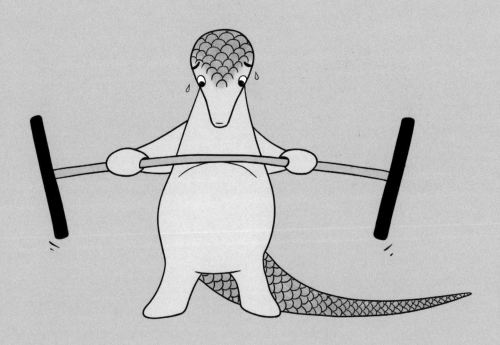

Best of all, find an exercise that makes you smile.

69 -w-

Prioritize spending
time in nature.

Discover beauty in the details.
The swirl of a snail, lines
of a leaf, buzz of a bee, and
a serendipitous encounter
. . . with a tasty snack.

If you are far from the forest, plant a tree or some flowers in a window box.

Pangolins are sometimes called gardeners of the forest. They keep ant and termite numbers under control by eating them, and they mix and aerate the soil as they dig for their food.

. . . or bring the forest into your home.

Grow a little every day . . .

and bloom.

It's okay to add "Do nothing" to your to-do list.

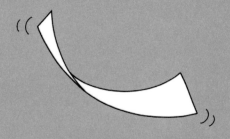

If you need to disguise
nothing as something,
try cloud watching.

Enjoy the restorative power of a hug.

Sometimes no words are needed to comfort a friend.

Not everyone enjoys time alone. Remind them that you care.

Female pangolins carry their pango pups on their backs. They stay together for up to two years before the young pangolins leave to live on their own.

If you send
a letter, you
might receive
one in return.

Be a good listener.

A pangolin's ears may not be the best for hearing, but they (and their nostrils too) can shut to stop ants from crawling into them.

**Keep in touch with
distant relatives.**

Xuyên Sơn, Vietnam

Akika, Nigeria

Agrawa, Ghana

Trenggiling, Indonesia

There are eight species of pangolins in the world,

Harakabvuka, Zimbabwe

Azhungu, India

Pipisin, Philippines

Kokolo, Central African Republic

four in Asia and four in Africa.

Do you fade as your device's battery fades? Recognize when you need to recharge.

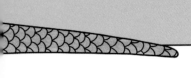

Find balance in life.

It's easier when you have a prehensile tail.

Stepping out of your comfort zone might be more fun than you expect.

Pangolins can swim, but not as well as otters.

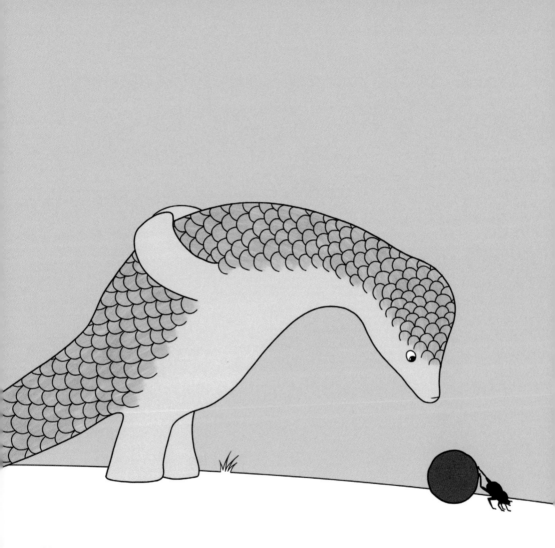

Sometimes even
the improbable can
be possible . . .

if you take one step at a time.

Choose the path most traveled,
the path least traveled,
or find your own way.

Be kind. Share your shelter.

Being solitary like a pangolin doesn't exclude you from sharing small acts of kindness with others.

Share your snacks.

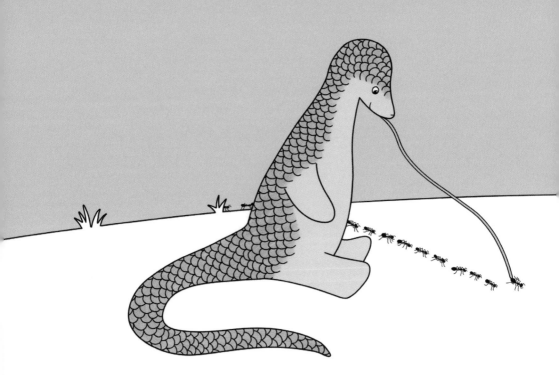

Pangolins eat ants, but they are not anteaters. Pangolins are more closely related to cats than to the anteaters of South America.

Don't try to be someone you're not. Be true to yourself.

Remember you're a pangolin, not a penguin.

When you're a pangolin,
you have to live for today.

Their tomorrow is up to us.

Resources

If you want to learn about pangolins and what you can do to help them, these websites are great places to get started:

* **SAVEPANGOLINS.ORG:** This nonprofit is dedicated to saving all eight pangolin species from extinction.

* **PANGOLINCRISISFUND.ORG:** The Pangolin Crisis Fund invests in projects to help pangolins and maintains a 100 percent donation model in which every dollar donated goes directly to pangolin-saving efforts.

* **PANGOLINSG.ORG:** The IUCN SSC Pangolin Specialist Group is dedicated to serving as a leader in global pangolin conservation.

To learn about the illegal trade in pangolins and other wildlife, I recommend reading *Poached: Inside the Dark World of Wildlife Trafficking* by Rachel Love Nuwer.

Acknowledgments

To the global community of pangolin conservationists who are so dedicated to saving pangolins from extinction, thank you for all you do and for sharing your knowledge and experience. Special thanks to those who sent me the local words for "pangolin" that became names of the characters in the video call illustration.

Thank you to everyone at Apollo Publishers for making this book a reality and especially to Julia Abramoff and Margaret Kaplan for their support, encouragement, and belief that pangolins should be better known.

I am forever grateful to Anna Maria Tan-Delfin and Joseph Pirmejo from Bookmark the Filipino Bookstore for publishing the first incarnation of Pipisin the pangolin.

Thank you to my husband and family for tolerating, and even encouraging, my obsession with an imaginary pangolin friend. And to my friends, in real life and online, who have liked my illustrations and offered encouraging words. Without you I would never have drawn quite so many pangolin pictures.

About the Author

RACHEL SHAW is an author and illustrator, and the communications officer for the Lincolnshire Wildlife Trust. In 2009, she was part of an exchange program organized between the UK and the Philippines by Rotary International and was able to see some of the incredible diversity of species on the country's 7,107 islands. As she learned more about the animals, she began to record their stories through text and artwork. Her children's book on pangolins was published in the Philippines in 2015 by The Bookmark, Inc. Today she is the creator of the heartwarming Instagram page @pipisinpangolin. She lives in Lincoln, UK.